44 Homemade Protein Shakes for Bodybuilders:

Increase Muscle Development without Pills, Creatine Supplements, or Anabolic Steroids

By Joseph Correa

Certified Sports Nutritionist

COPYRIGHT

© 2016 Correa Media Group

All rights reserved

Reproduction or translation of any part of this work beyond that permitted by section 107 or 108 of the 1976 United States Copyright Act without the permission of the copyright owner is unlawful.

This publication is designed to provide accurate and authoritative information in regard to the subject matter covered. It is sold with the understanding that neither the author nor the publisher is engaged in rendering medical advice. If medical advice or assistance is needed, consult with a doctor. This book is considered a guide and should not be used in any way detrimental to your health. Consult with a physician before starting this nutritional plan to make sure it's right for you.

ACKNOWLEDGEMENTS

The realization and success of this book could not have been possible without my family.

44 Homemade Protein Shakes for Bodybuilders:

Increase Muscle Development without Pills, Creatine Supplements, or Anabolic Steroids

By Joseph Correa

Certified Sports Nutritionist

CONTENTS

Copyright

Acknowledgements

About The Author

Introduction

44 Homemade Protein Shakes for Bodybuilders

Other Great Titles by This Author

ABOUT THE AUTHOR

As a certified sports nutritionist and professional athlete, I firmly believe that proper nutrition will help you reach your goals faster and effectively. My knowledge and experience has helped me live healthier throughout the years and which I have shared with family and friends. The more you know about eating and drinking healthier, the sooner you will want to change your life and eating habits.

Being successful in controlling your weight is important as it will improve all aspects of your life.

Nutrition is a key part in the process of getting in better shape and that's what this book is all about.

INTRODUCTION

44 Homemade Protein Shakes for Bodybuilders will help you increase the amount of protein you consume per day to help increase muscle mass. These meals will help increase muscle in an organized manner by adding large healthy portions of protein to your diet. Being too busy to eat right can sometimes become a problem and that's why this book will save you time and help nourish your body to achieve the goals you want. Make sure you know what you're eating by preparing it yourself or having someone prepare it for you.

This book will help you to:

-Gain muscle fast naturally.

-Improve muscle recovery.

-Have more energy.

-Naturally accelerate Your Metabolism to build more muscle.

-Improve your digestive system.

Joseph Correa is a certified sports nutritionist and a professional athlete.

44 HOMEMADE PROTEIN SHAKES FOR BODYBUILDERS

1. Tomato protein shake:

Ingredients:

1 glass of skim milk

¼ tsp of cinnamon

1 small tomato

1 grated carrot

1 tsp of brown sugar

Preparation:

Wash and cut tomato into small cubes. Peel and grate the carrot. You want to cut the carrot into thin strips. Mix the ingredients in a blender and keep in the refrigerator.

Nutritional values for 1 glass:

Carbohydrates 10.9g

Sugar 7.85g

Protein 4.38g

Total fat 2.31g

Sodium 84mg

Potassium 423mg

Calcium 283.7mg

Iron 0.832mg

Vitamins (Vitamin C total ascorbic acid; B-6; B-12; Folate-DFE; A-RAE; A-IU; E-alpha-tocopherol; D; D-D2+D3; Thianin; Niacin)

Calories 80

2. Vegetable protein shake

Ingredients:

1 cup of chopped broccoli

half bunch of fresh spinach

½ cup of low fat yogurt

1 tsp of honey

few leaves of mint

¼ cup of water

Preparation:

Wash the vegetables and put into a blender. Put some ice cubes and blend together until smooth mixture.

Nutritional values for 1 glass:

Carbohydrates 12.32g

Sugar 7.16g

Protein 4.95g

Total fat 2.78g

Sodium 79mg

Potassium 243.6mg

Calcium 117mg

Iron 2.65mg

Vitamins (Vitamin C total ascorbic acid; B-6; B-12; Folate-DFE; A-RAE; A-IU; E-alpha-tocopherol; D; D-D2+D3; K-phylloquinone; Thianin; Riboflavin; Niacin)

Calories 81.3

3. Mixed fruits and vegetables protein shake

Ingredients:

1 cup of mixed blueberries, raspberries, blackberries and strawberries

½ cup of chopped baby spinach

2 egg whites

½ cup of low fat yogurt

1.5 glass of water

Preparation:

Wash the baby spinach and put it in a blender. Mix 2 egg whites with low fat yogurt, add water and put in a blender. Add mixed fruits and mix for few minutes.

Nutritional values for 1 glass:

Carbohydrates 11.27g

Sugar 8.11g

Protein 5.85g

Total fat 2.94g

Sodium 85mg

Potassium 259.6mg

Calcium 113mg

Iron 2.03mg

Vitamins (Vitamin C total ascorbic acid; B-6; B-12; Folate-DFE; A-RAE; A-IU; E-alpha-tocopherol; D; D-D2+D3; K-phylloquinone; Thianin; Riboflavin; Niacin)

Calories 72.6

4. Melon protein shake

Ingredients:

¼ cup of fresh strawberries

¼ of banana

1 slice of melon

½ tsp of cinnamon

¼ cup of chopped walnuts

1 tsp of brown sugar

Preparation:

Mix ingredients in a blender and sprinkle with cinnamon. Keep in the refrigerator and serve cold.

Nutritional values for 1 glass:

Carbohydrates 13.24g

Sugar 9.19g

Protein 7.92g

Total fat 3.54g

Sodium 91mg

Potassium 273.6mg

Calcium 119mg

Iron 2.09mg

Vitamins (Vitamin C total ascorbic acid; B-6; B-12; Folate-DFE; A-RAE; A-IU; E-alpha-tocopherol; D; D-D2+D3; K-phylloquinone; Thianin; Riboflavin; Niacin)

Calories 78

5. Strawberries protein shake:

Ingredients:

1 cup of strawberries

½ cup of skim milk

1 tsp of agave syrup

Preparation:

Mix the ingredients in a blender for few minutes. Leave it in the refrigerator for few minutes and serve cold. You can add some ice cubes in it.

Nutritional values for 1 glass:

Carbohydrates 8.19g

Sugar 4.05g

Protein 4.97g

Total fat 2.64g

Sodium 62mg

Potassium 197.9mg

Calcium 111mg

Iron 1.23mg

Vitamins (Vitamin C; B-6; B-12; E-alpha-tocopherol; D; D-D2+D3; K-phylloquinone; Thianin; Riboflavin; Niacin)

Calories 54

6. Vanilla protein shake

Ingredients:

1 glass of skim milk

½ glass of water

1 tsp of vanilla extract

1 tsp of minced vanilla

¼ tsp of cinnamon

2 tsp of brown sugar

Preparation:

Mix the milk with water and boil on a low temperature. Add minced vanilla and vanilla extract. Stir well and let it boil for about a minute. Remove from the heath and allow it to cool. Mix with another ingredients in a blender for few minutes. Serve cold.

Nutritional values for 1 glass:

Carbohydrates 10.12g

Sugar 6.05g

Protein 4.66g

Total fat 1.65g

Sodium 79mg

Potassium 203.4mg

Calcium 92mg

Iron 1.98mg

Vitamins (Vitamin C total ascorbic acid; B-6; B-12; Folate-DFE; A-RAE; A-IU; D; D-D2+D3; K-phylloquinone; Thianin; Riboflavin; Niacin)

Calories 79

7. Broccoli protein shake

Ingredients:

1 cup of cooked broccoli

1 glass of water

1 cup of goji berries

1 tsp of brown sugar

Preparation:

Mix the ingredients in a blender for few minutes. Serve this healthy drink cold.

Nutritional values for 1 glass:

Carbohydrates 9.31g

Sugar 5.19g

Protein 4.83g

Total fat 1.67g

Sodium 78mg

Potassium 201mg

Calcium 86mg

Iron 1.13mg

Vitamins (Vitamin C total ascorbic acid; B-6; B-12; A-RAE; A-IU; D; D-D2+D3; K-phylloquinone; Thianin; Riboflavin; Niacin)

Calories 68.3

8. Coffee protein shake

Ingredients:

1 cup of unsweetened chilled coffee

½ cup of skim milk

2 tsp of vanilla extract

2 tsp of brown sugar

1 tbsp of Greek yogurt

cinnamon (optional).

Preparation:

Combine all the ingredients in a blender. Mix well for about 30 seconds. Drink cold. You can add some cinnamon on top, but this is optional. Keep this protein shake in the refrigerator, or you can even freeze it for later use.

Nutritional values for 1 glass:

Carbohydrates 8.54g

Sugar 5.73g

Protein 8.78g

Total fat 2.04g

Sodium 69mg

Potassium 227mg

Calcium 117mg

Iron 2.79mg

Vitamins (Vitamin C total ascorbic acid; B-6; B-12; Folate-DFE; A-RAE; A-IU; D; D-D2+D3; K-phylloquinone; Thianin; Riboflavin; Niacin)

Calories 71.3

9. Apple and orange protein shake

Ingredients:

- 1 small apple
- 1 small orange
- ½ glass of water
- 1 tsp of brown sugar
- 1 tsp of honey
- 1 tsp of chopped almonds

Preparation:

Put all the ingredients in a blender for few minutes. Drink cold.

Nutritional values for 1 glass:

Carbohydrates 12.31g

Sugar 8.73g

Protein 6.98g

Total fat 3.09g

Sodium 81mg

Potassium 265.9mg

Calcium 109mg

Iron 1.54mg

Vitamins (Vitamin C total ascorbic acid; B-6; B-12; Folate-DFE; A-RAE; A-IU; E-alpha-tocopherol; D; D-D2+D3; K-phylloquinone; Thianin; Riboflavin; Niacin)

Calories 73.1

10. Fruit shake

Ingredients:

1 cup of blueberries

1 banana

½ tsp of cinnamon

½ glass of skim milk

1 tbsp of agave syrup

Preparation:

Peel the banana and cut into small pieces. Combine agave syrup with skim milk and boil briefly. Allow it to cool for a while. Mix the ingredients in a blender for about 30 seconds. Sprinkle with cinnamon and serve cold.

Nutritional values for one glass:

Carbohydrates 11.12g

Sugar 9.34g

Protein 6.52g

Total fat 3.21g

Sodium 93mg

Potassium 208.31mg

Calcium 113mg

Iron 3.21mg

Vitamins (Vitamin C total ascorbic acid; B-6; B-12; Folate-DFE; A-RAE; A-IU; E-alpha-tocopherol; D; D-D2+D3; K-phylloquinone; Thianin; Riboflavin; Niacin)

Calories 79.9

11. Oatmeal protein shake

Ingredients:

½ cups of oatmeal

1 cup of skim milk

¼ cup of water

1 tsp of vanilla extract

½ banana

Preparation:

This recipes takes only few minutes to prepare and it is super tasty. All you want to do is combine the ingredients in a blender and mix until smooth mixture for about 30-40 seconds. Leave in the refrigerator for 30 minutes. You can sprinkle some cinnamon on top.

Nutritional values for 1 glass:

Carbohydrates 13.32g

Sugar 7.17g

Protein 6.91g

Total fat 3.99g

Sodium 92mg

Potassium 263.2mg

Calcium 119mg

Iron 2.92mg

Vitamins (Vitamin C total ascorbic acid; B-6; B-12; Folate-DFE; A-RAE; A-IU; D; D-D2+D3; K-phylloquinone; Thianin; Riboflavin)

Calories 89

12. Peppermint protein shake

Ingredients:

2 cups of skim milk

1 tsp of cocoa powder

1 tsp of grated almonds

1 tbsp of fat free cream

½ tsp of peppermint extract

Preparation:

Boil the milk on a low temperature. Add peppermint extract and cocoa powder. Stir well for 2-3 minutes. Remove from the heath and allow it to cool for about 30 minutes. Now mix with the grated almonds and fat free cream and put in a blender for about 30 seconds.

Nutritional values for 1 glass:

Carbohydrates 10.32g

Sugar 7.34g

Protein 6.81g

Total fat 3.08g

Sodium 85.9mg

Potassium 243.3mg

Calcium 121mg

Iron 1.09mg

Vitamins (Vitamin C total ascorbic acid; B-6; B-12; Folate-DFE; A-RAE; A-IU; E-alpha-tocopherol; D; D-D2+D3; K-phylloquinone; Thianin; Riboflavin; Niacin)

Calories 68.2

13. Flaxseed oil protein shake

Ingredients:

½ cup of water

½ cup of skim milk

1 tbsp of grated walnuts

1 tbsp of goji berries

1 tbsp of flaxseed oil

1 tsp of vanilla extract

1 tbsp of brown sugar

Preparation:

Mix the ingredients in a blender for about 40 seconds, or until smooth mixture. Keep in the refrigerator and serve cold.

Nutritional values for 1 glass:

Carbohydrates 14.31g

Sugar 9.19g

Protein 7.81g

Total fat 3.09g

Sodium 83mg

Potassium 279.9mg

Calcium 129mg

Iron 3.09mg

Vitamins (Vitamin C total ascorbic acid; B-6; B-12; Folate-DFE; A-RAE; A-IU; E-alpha-tocopherol; D; D-D2+D3; K-phylloquinone; Thianin; Riboflavin; Niacin)

Calories 113

14. Cinnamon protein shake

Ingredients:

1 glass of skim milk

1 tsp of cocoa powder

1 tbsp of raisins

1 tbsp of pumpkin seeds

¼ tsp of cinnamon

Preparation:

Mix in a blender until smooth mixture. Serve with ice cubes. You can sprinkle some more cinnamon on top before serving.

Nutritional values for 1 glass:

Carbohydrates 12.9g

Sugar 9.27g

Protein 7.75g

Total fat 4.57g

Sodium 92.3mg

Potassium 262.7mg

Calcium 123.5mg

Iron 5.21mg

Vitamins (Vitamin C total ascorbic acid; B-6; B-12; Folate-DFE; A-RAE; A-IU; E-alpha-tocopherol; D; D-D2+D3; K-phylloquinone; Thianin; Riboflavin; Niacin)

Calories 86.7

15. Almond protein shake

Ingredients:

1 cup of skim milk

½ cup of water

2 egg whites

1 tbsp of grated almonds

1 tbsp of honey

½ cup of oatmeal

Preparation:

Separate the egg whites from the yolks. Combine with other ingredients and mix in a blender for 30-40 seconds. Allow it to cool in the refrigerator. Serve cold.

Nutritional values for 1 glass:

Carbohydrates 14.31g

Sugar 9.19g

Protein 7.91g

Total fat 4.54g

Sodium 103mg

Potassium 287.9mg

Calcium 122mg

Iron 4.29mg

Vitamins (Vitamin C; B-6; B-12; Folate-DFE; A-RAE; A-IU; E-alpha-tocopherol; D; D-D2+D3; K; Thianin; Riboflavin; Niacin)

Calories 91

16. Banana protein shake

Ingredients:

1 large banana

1 cup of skim milk

½ cup of water

1 tsp of vanilla extract

1 tbsp of agave syrup

Preparation:

Peel and chop banana into small cubes. Combine with other ingredients in a blender and mix for 30 seconds, until smooth mixture. Keep in the refrigerator and serve cold.

Nutritional values for 1 glass:

Carbohydrates 10.11g

Sugar 7.17g

Protein 8.91g

Total fat 3.23g

Sodium 95mg

Potassium 612.9mg

Calcium 119mg

Iron 2.88mg

Vitamins (Vitamin C total ascorbic acid; B-6; B-12; Folate-DFE; A-RAE; A-IU; E-alpha-tocopherol; D; D-D2+D3; K-phylloquinone; Thianin; Riboflavin; Niacin)

Calories 88

17. Bran flakes protein shake

Ingredients:

1 cup of skim milk

½ cup of water

½ cup of bran flakes

1 tbsp of brown sugar

1 tbsp of honey

1 tsp of cocoa

Preparation:

Mix in a blender for 30-40 seconds, or until smooth mixture. You can add some cinnamon, but this is optional. Allow it to cool in the refrigerator for about an hour. Serve cold.

Nutritional values for 1 glass:

Carbohydrates 11.7g

Sugar 10.01g

Protein 5.32g

Total fat 3.65g

Sodium 86.5mg

Potassium 262mg

Calcium 111mg

Iron 3.75mg

Vitamins (Vitamin C total ascorbic acid; B-6; B-12; Folate-DFE; A-RAE; A-IU; E;D; D-D2+D3; K-phylloquinone; Thianin; Riboflavin)

Calories 78.7

18. Wild berries protein shake

Ingredients:

½ cup of wild berries

½ cup of fresh wild berries juice

½ cup of water

1 tsp of blackberry extract

2 egg whites

1 handful of ice

Preparation:

Separate the egg whites from the yolks. Combine with other ingredients and mix in a blender for about 30 seconds. Serve cold.

Nutritional values for 1 glass:

Carbohydrates 13.01g

Sugar 9g

Protein 7.8g

Total fat 1.95g

Sodium 98mg

Potassium 234.7mg

Calcium 110mg

Iron 3.04mg

Vitamins (Vitamin C total ascorbic acid; B-6; B-12; Folate-DFE; A-RAE; A-IU; E-alpha-tocopherol; D; D-D2+D3; K-phylloquinone; Thianin; Riboflavin; Niacin)

Calories 68

19. Walnuts protein shake

Ingredients:

1 cup of coconut milk

½ cup of grated walnuts

½ cup of finely chopped spinach

1 whole egg

2 tbsp of brown sugar

1 tsp of walnut extract

Preparation:

Combine the ingredients in a blender and mix for 30-40 seconds. Add some ice cubes before serving.

Nutritional values for 1 glass:

Carbohydrates 11.27g

Sugar 8.11g

Protein 5.85g

Total fat 2.94g

Sodium 85mg

Potassium 259.6mg

Calcium 113mg

Iron 2.03mg

Vitamins (Vitamin C total ascorbic acid; B-6; B-12; Folate-DFE; A-RAE; A-IU; E-alpha-tocopherol; D; D-D2+D3; K-phylloquinone; Thianin; Riboflavin; Niacin)

Calories 72.6

20. Greek yogurt protein shake

Ingredients:

1 cup of Greek yogurt

1 tbsp of honey

1 tbsp of brown sugar

¼ cup of skim milk

1 tsp of almond butter

¼ tsp of cinnamon

Preparation:

Combine the milk, almond butter and brown sugar in a saucepan. Stir well and allow it to boil, on a low temperature for about 2 minutes. Remove from the heath and cool for 15 minutes. Pour the mixture in a blender and add other ingredients. Mix well for 30-40 seconds and keep in the refrigerator to cool.

Nutritional values for 1 glass:

Carbohydrates 13.1g

Sugar 9g

Protein 7.91g

Total fat 3.03g

Sodium 95mg

Potassium 259mg

Calcium 119mg

Iron 3mg

Vitamins (Vitamin C total ascorbic acid; B-6; B-12; Folate-DFE; A-RAE; A-IU; E-alpha-tocopherol; D; D-D2+D3; K-phylloquinone; Thianin; Riboflavin; Niacin)

Calories 70

21. Protein shake with eggs

Ingredients:

1 cup of skim milk

½ cup of water

1 tbsp of Greek yogurt

3 eggs

1 tsp of vanilla extract

1 tbsp of brown sugar

Preparation:

Combine the ingredients in a blender and mix until smooth mixture. Serve cold.

Nutritional values for 1 glass:

Carbohydrates 10g

Sugar 6.02g

Protein 9.84g

Total fat 3.94g

Sodium 95mg

Potassium 212.2mg

Calcium 123mg

Iron 2.43mg

Vitamins (Vitamin C;B-6; B-12; Folate-DFE; A-RAE; A-IU; D; D-D2+D3; K-phylloquinone; Thianin; Riboflavin; Niacin)

Calories 72

22. Peanut butter protein shake

Ingredients:

1 cup of skim milk

¼ cup of finely chopped peanuts

1 tbsp of peanut butter

1 tbsp of brown sugar

1 tbsp of goji berries

1 small green apple

Preparation:

Peel and chop the apple into thin slices. Use a saucepan to melt the peanut butter on a low temperature. Add brown sugar and stir well for 30 seconds. Remove from the heath and allow it to cool. Meanwhile, mix the other ingredients in a blender, add peanut and sugar and mix well for 30-40 seconds. Keep in the refrigerator for at least 30 minutes to cool.

Nutritional values for 1 glass:

Carbohydrates 13.2g

Sugar 10.7g

Protein 11.6g

Total fat 2.8g

Sodium 97mg

Potassium 259mg

Calcium 134.3mg

Iron 3.09mg

Vitamins (Vitamin C total ascorbic acid; B-6; B-12; Folate-DFE; A-RAE; A-IU; E-alpha-tocopherol; D; D-D2+D3; K-phylloquinone; Thianin; Riboflavin; Niacin)

Calories 88.4

23. Energy protein shake

Ingredients:

1 tbsp of grated almonds

1 tbsp of grated walnuts

1 tbsp of grated macadamian nuts

1 cup of aronia

1 medium banana

1 glass of fresh orange juice

1 glass of water

2 egg whites

2 tbsp of honey

1 tbsp of brown sugar

Preparation:

This protein shake is very easy to prepare. Simply combine the ingredients in a blender and mix well for 40 seconds. Cool well before serving.

Nutritional values for 1 glass:

Carbohydrates 17.47g

Sugar 14.03g

Protein 15.8g

Total fat 7.94g

Sodium 175mg

Potassium 369mg

Calcium 189mg

Iron 6.09mg

Vitamins (Vitamin C total ascorbic acid; B-6; B-12; Folate-DFE; A-RAE; A-IU; E-alpha-tocopherol; D; D-D2+D3; K-phylloquinone; Thianin; Riboflavin; Niacin)

Calories 149

24. Pistachio protein shake

Ingredients:

1 cup of skim milk

¼ cup of finely chopped pistachios

1 tbsp of peanut butter

1 tbsp of honey

1 handful of ice

Preparation:

Mix the ingredients in a blender until smooth mixture.

Nutritional values for 1 glass:

Carbohydrates 13.4g

Sugar 9.15g

Protein 7.81g

Total fat 5.91g

Sodium 105mg

Potassium 287mg

Calcium 115mg

Iron 3.03mg

Vitamins (Vitamin C total ascorbic acid; B-6; B-12; Folate-DFE; A-RAE; A-IU; E-alpha-tocopherol; D; D-D2+D3; K-phylloquinone; Thianin; Riboflavin; Niacin)

Calories 81

25. Almond butter protein shake

Ingredients:

1 cup of skim milk

½ cup of water

½ cup of oatmeal

1 tbsp of brown sugar

2 tbsp of almond butter

1 tsp of almond extract

¼ cup of almond milk

Preparation:

Boil the almond milk on a low temperature. Add almond extract, almond butter and brown sugar. Stir well and allow it to boil for 30-40 seconds. Remove from the heath and cool. Combine with other ingredients in a blender and mix well for 30 seconds. Serve cold.

Nutritional values for 1 glass:

Carbohydrates 15.3g

Sugar 8.11g

Protein 9.83g

Total fat 7.81g

Sodium 106mg

Potassium 297.2mg

Calcium 125mg

Iron 4.09mg

Vitamins (Vitamin C total ascorbic acid; B-6; B-12; Folate-DFE; A-RAE; A-IU; E-alpha-tocopherol; D; D-D2+D3; K-phylloquinone; Thianin; Riboflavin; Niacin)

Calories 73

26. Green apples protein shake

Ingredients:

1 green apple

2 egg whites

1 glass of fresh apple juice

1 tbsp of grated walnuts

¼ tsp of cinnamon

Preparation:

Peel and cut the apple into thin slices. Separate egg whites from the yolks. Mix with other ingredients in a blender for 30-40 seconds. Serve with ice cubes.

Nutritional values for 1 glass:

Carbohydrates 11g

Sugar 8g

Protein 8.92g

Total fat 3.44g

Sodium 92mg

Potassium 212.4mg

Calcium 103mg

Iron 3.03mg

Vitamins (Vitamin C total ascorbic acid; B-6; B-12; Folate-DFE; A-RAE; A-IU; E-alpha-tocopherol; D; D-D2+D3; K-phylloquinone; Thianin; Riboflavin; Niacin)

Calories 62

27. Honey and banana protein shake

Ingredients:

1 cup of skim milk

1 medium banana

1 tbsp of honey

1 tsp of banana extract

1 tbsp of Greek yogurt

1 tbsp of non fat cream

Preparation:

Peel and chop banana into small cubes. Mix with other ingredients in a blender for 30-40 seconds and allow it to cool in the refrigerator for about an hour. Serve cold.

Nutritional values for 1 glass:

Carbohydrates 12.7g

Sugar 7.1g

Protein 9.92g

Total fat 2.94g

Sodium 85mg

Potassium 249.5mg

Calcium 133mg

Iron 3mg

Vitamins (Vitamin C total ascorbic acid; B-6; B-12; Folate-DFE; A-RAE; A-IU; E-alpha-tocopherol; D; D-D2+D3; K-phylloquinone; Thianin; Riboflavin; Niacin)

Calories 68.9

28. Mixed nuts protein shake

Ingredients:

1 tsp of grated almonds

1 tsp of grated walnuts

1 tsp of grated hazelnuts

1 tsp of grated macadamian nuts

1 glass of fresh orange juice

1 tbsp of agave syrup

1 tbsp of non fat orange ice cream

1 handful of ice cubes

Preparation:

Mix the ingredients in a blender for 30-40 seconds.

Nutritional values for 1 glass:

Carbohydrates 15.19g

Sugar 11.23g

Protein 9.85g

Total fat 6.64g

Sodium 115mg

Potassium 309.6mg

Calcium 121mg

Iron 5.03mg

Vitamins (Vitamin C total ascorbic acid; B-6; B-12; Folate-DFE; A-RAE; A-IU; E-alpha-tocopherol; D; D-D2+D3; K-phylloquinone; Thianin; Riboflavin; Niacin)

Calories 98.3

29. Pineapple protein shake

Ingredients:

1 cup of chopped fresh pineapple

1 cup of fresh pineapple juice

2 egg whites

1 tbsp of brown sugar

1 tsp of pineapple extract

2 cherries for decoration

Preparation:

Separate the egg whites from the yolk. Mix with other ingredients in a blender for 30-40 seconds. Serve with ice and cherries on top.

Nutritional values for 1 glass:

Carbohydrates 11.34g

Sugar 8.11g

Protein 6.85g

Total fat 1.84g

Sodium 84mg

Potassium 209.6mg

Calcium 103mg

Iron 1.93mg

Vitamins (Vitamin C total ascorbic acid; B-6; B-12; Folate-DFE; A-RAE; A-IU; E-alpha-tocopherol; D; D-D2+D3; K-phylloquinone; Thianin; Riboflavin; Niacin)

Calories 58.9

30. Exotic protein shake

Ingredients:

1 cup of coconut milk

½ banana

½ cup of chopped pineapple

1 tsp of coconut extract

2 tbsp of low-fat sour cream

2 tbsp of brown sugar

Preparation:

Combine the ingredients in a blender for 30-40 seconds and mix well until smooth mixture. Serve with some ice cubes.

Nutritional values for 1 glass:

Carbohydrates 11.17g

Sugar 8.31g

Protein 5.85g

Total fat 2.44g

Sodium 82mg

Potassium 279.6mg

Calcium 114mg

Iron 2.3mg

Vitamins (Vitamin C total ascorbic acid; B-6; B-12; Folate-DFE; A-RAE; A-IU; E-alpha-tocopherol; D; D-D2+D3; K-phylloquinone; Thianin; Riboflavin; Niacin)

Calories 72

31. Peach and cream protein shake

Ingredients:

1 medium peach

1 glass of almond milk

1 tbsp of low-fat sour cream

1 tbsp of Greek yogurt

1 tsp of peach extract

1 tbsp of honey

1 tsp of pumpkin seeds

1 handful of ice

Preparation:

Cut the peach into small pieces. Mix with other ingredients in a blender until smooth mixture.

Nutritional values for 1 glass:

Carbohydrates 13.27g

Sugar 9.11g

Protein 7.85g

Total fat 4.94g

Sodium 85mg

Potassium 259mg

Calcium 103mg

Iron 2.93mg

Vitamins (Vitamin C total ascorbic acid; B-6; B-12; Folate-DFE; A-RAE; A-IU; E-alpha-tocopherol; D; D-D2+D3; K-phylloquinone; Thianin; Riboflavin; Niacin)

Calories 70

32. Greek vanilla yogurt protein shake

Ingredients:

1 cup of Greek vanilla yogurt

1 cup of skim milk

1 tbsp of grated macadamia nuts

1 medium banana

½ cup of strawberries

1 tsp of vanilla extract

Preparation:

Peel the banana and cut into small cubes. Combine with the other ingredients in a blender and mix until smooth mixture, about 30-40 seconds. You can sprinkle some vanilla powder on top, but this is optional. Serve cold.

Nutritional values for 1 glass:

Carbohydrates 12.2g

Sugar 6.1g

Protein 9.85g

Total fat 3.4g

Sodium 79mg

Potassium 216.6mg

Calcium 111mg

Iron 2.3mg

Vitamins (Vitamin C total ascorbic acid; B-6; B-12; Folate-DFE; A-RAE; A-IU; E-alpha-tocopherol; D; D-D2+D3; K-phylloquinone; Thianin; Riboflavin; Niacin)

Calories 78

33. Plum power shake

Ingredients:

3 ripe plums, pitted

1 cup of skim milk

½ cup of walnuts

¼ cup of agave syrup

Preparation:

Mix the ingredients in a blender for 30-40 seconds. Serve cold.

Nutritional values for 1 glass:

Carbohydrates 12.21g

Sugar 5.98g

Protein 6.23g

Total fat 2.31g

Sodium 82.5mg

Potassium 217.8mg

Calcium 124.3mg

Iron 1.27mg

Vitamins (Vitamin C total ascorbic acid; B-6; B-12; Folate-DFE; A-RAE; A-IU; E-alpha-tocopherol; D; D-D2+D3; K-phylloquinone; Thianin; Riboflavin; Niacin)

Calories 56.4

34. Lemon protein shake

Ingredients:

1 glass of fresh lemonade, without sugar

1 tbsp of lemon zest

2 tbsp of brown sugar

½ cup of cottage cheese

1 tbsp of vanilla extract

1 tbsp of grated oat crackers

Preparation:

Put the ingredients into a blender and blend until you get a creamy consistency. Pour it in a glass and sprinkle with grated oat crackers. Serve cold.

Nutritional values for 1 glass:

Carbohydrates 9.27g

Sugar 6.11g

Protein 8.85g

Total fat 4.94g

Sodium 86mg

Potassium 211.4mg

Calcium 115mg

Iron 1.05mg

Vitamins (Vitamin C total ascorbic acid; B-6; B-12; Folate-DFE; A-RAE; A-IU; E-alpha-tocopherol; D; D-D2+D3; K-phylloquinone; Thianin; Riboflavin; Niacin)

Calories 57.6

35. Caramel protein shake

Ingredients:

1 cup of skim milk

½ cup of brown sugar

½ tsp of cinnamon

1 tsp of chocolate extract

1 tbsp of grated almonds

1 medium pear, chopped into small pieces

2 tbsp of Greek yogurt

Preparation:

Use a saucepan to melt the sugar on a low temperature. Slowly add the milk and stir well for about a minute. Your sugar will become a nice caramel. Remove from the heath and allow it to cool for a while. Meanwhile cut a pear into small pieces, combine with other ingredients in a blender, add caramel and blend for about 40 seconds. Pour the protein shake into a glass, sprinkle with cinnamon and add some ice cubes.

Nutritional values for 1 glass:

Carbohydrates 12.37g

Sugar 8.42g

Protein 6.85g

Total fat 2.74g

Sodium 83mg

Potassium 239.6mg

Calcium 112mg

Iron 2.05mg

Vitamins (Vitamin C total ascorbic acid; B-6; B-12; Folate-DFE; A-RAE; A-IU; E-alpha-tocopherol; D; D-D2+D3; K-phylloquinone; Thianin; Riboflavin; Niacin)

Calories 72.7

36. Hazelnuts protein shake

Ingredients:

1 cup of skim milk

½ cup of chocolate Greek yogurt

1 tsp of cocoa powder

2 tbsp of grated hazelnuts

1 tbsp of brown sugar

2 egg whites

Preparation:

Combine the ingredients in a blender and mix until creamy mixture. Allow it to cool in the refrigerator for about 30 minutes.

Nutritional values for 1 glass:

Carbohydrates 11.27g

Sugar 8.13g

Protein 9.84g

Total fat 2.94g

Sodium 82mg

Potassium 253.6mg

Calcium 112mg

Iron 2.08mg

Vitamins (Vitamin C total ascorbic acid; B-6; B-12; Folate-DFE; A-RAE; A-IU; E-alpha-tocopherol; D; D-D2+D3; K-phylloquinone; Thianin; Riboflavin; Niacin)

Calories 62.6

37. Chocolate and coffee protein shake

Ingredients:

1 cup of strong black coffee, without sugar

½ cup of low-fat cream

3 tbsp of Greek yogurt

1 tbsp of brown sugar

1 tsp of cocoa

¼ cup of grated dark chocolate (80% of cocoa)

1 tbsp of grated hazelnuts

Preparation:

Mix the ingredients in a blender for 30-40 seconds. Keep in the refrigerator and serve with ice cubes. Sprinkle some grated hazelnuts on top.

Nutritional values for 1 glass:

Carbohydrates 15.27g

Sugar 8.51g

Protein 10.83g

Total fat 6.94g

Sodium 83mg

Potassium 259.3mg

Calcium 143mg

Iron 2.23mg

Vitamins (Vitamin C total ascorbic acid; B-6; B-12; Folate-DFE; A-RAE; A-IU; E-alpha-tocopherol; D; D-D2+D3; K-phylloquinone; Thianin; Riboflavin; Niacin)

Calories 74

38. Cherry protein shake

Ingredients:

1 cup of fresh cherry juice, without sugar

1 cup of cherries

½ cup of Greek yogurt

1 tsp of cherry extract

1 tbsp of brown sugar

1 handful of ice

Preparation:

You just need to mix the ingredients in a blender for 30 seconds. Serve cold.

Nutritional values for 1 glass:

Carbohydrates 10.67g

Sugar 8.11g

Protein 8.65g

Total fat 2.54g

Sodium 95mg

Potassium 159.6mg

Calcium 93mg

Iron 1.03mg

Vitamins (Vitamin C total ascorbic acid; B-6; B-12; A-RAE; A-IU; E-alpha-tocopherol; D; K-phylloquinone; Thianin; Riboflavin; Niacin)

Calories 74.6

39. Mango protein shake

Ingredients:

1 cup of chopped mango

½ cup of oatmeal

1 tsp of pumpkin seeds

1 tsp of almond butter

1 cup of skim milk

1 tbsp of low-fat cream

2 tbsp of brown sugar

Preparation:

Combine the ingredients and blend until incorporated. Top with some mango extract powder, but this is optional. Serve cold.

Nutritional values for 1 glass:

Carbohydrates 14.24g

Sugar 8.11g

Protein 10.85g

Total fat 6.94g

Sodium 75mg

Potassium 249.6mg

Calcium 103mg

Iron 2.93mg

Vitamins (Vitamin C total ascorbic acid; B-6; B-12; Folate-DFE; A-RAE; A-IU; E-alpha-tocopherol; D; D-D2+D3; K-phylloquinone; Thianin; Riboflavin; Niacin)

Calories 82.6

40. Forest pleasure protein shake

Ingredients:

1 cup of fresh apple juice

½ cup of water

½ medium green apple

½ medium carrot

½ small peach

½ cup of mixed forest berries (raspberries, strawberries, blackberries)

½ cup of cottage cheese

1 tbsp of agave syrup

Preparation:

Mix in a blender until smooth mixture. Allow it to cool in the refrigerator for a while.

Nutritional values for 1 glass:

Carbohydrates 11.27g

Sugar 8.41g

Protein 9.85g

Total fat 4.94g

Sodium 84mg

Potassium 159.6mg

Calcium 84mg

Iron 1.3mg

Vitamins (Vitamin C total ascorbic acid; B-6; B-12; Folate-DFE; A-RAE; A-IU; E-alpha-tocopherol; D; D-D2+D3; K-phylloquinone; Thianin; Riboflavin; Niacin)

Calories 59

41. Ginger protein shake

Ingredients:

1 medium banana

1 cup of low-fat yogurt

1 cup of finely chopped spinach

1 tsp of grated ginger

2 egg whites

1 tsp of lemon juice

2 tbsp of honey

Preparation:

Separate egg whites from yolks. Mix with other ingredients in a blender for about 30 seconds, until foamy mixture.

Nutritional values for 1 glass:

Carbohydrates 10g

Sugar 5.11g

Protein 9.85g

Total fat 4.94g

Sodium 83mg

Potassium 229.6mg

Calcium 115mg

Iron 2.13mg

Vitamins (Vitamin C total ascorbic acid; B-6; B-12; Folate-DFE; A-RAE; A-IU; E-alpha-tocopherol; D; D-D2+D3; K-phylloquinone; Thianin; Riboflavin; Niacin)

Calories 74.6

42. Papaya protein shake

Ingredients:

1 cup of papaya puree

½ cup of oatmeal

1 cup of skim milk

½ cup of water

1 tbsp of goji berries

1 tbsp of agave syrup

2 tbsp of brown sugar

Preparation:

Combine the ingredients in a blender and mix well until smooth mixture. Serve with some ice cubes.

Nutritional values for 1 glass:

Carbohydrates 11.2g

Sugar 7.11g

Protein 9.85g

Total fat 2.44g

Sodium 84mg

Potassium 178.6mg

Calcium 113mg

Iron 2.03mg

Vitamins (Vitamin C total ascorbic acid; B-6; B-12; Folate-DFE; A-RAE; A-IU; E-alpha-tocopherol; D; D-D2+D3; K-phylloquinone; Thianin; Riboflavin; Niacin)

Calories 69.5

43. Blueberries protein shake

Ingredients:

1 cup of skim milk

1 cup of blueberries

1 tbsp of brown sugar

1 tsp of mint extract

Preparation:

Very simple to prepare. This protein is very refreshing and it only takes about 2-3 minutes to prepare it. Just mix the ingredients in a blender for 30 seconds and serve with ice cubes.

Nutritional values for 1 glass:

Carbohydrates 7g

Sugar 3.11g

Protein 5.8g

Total fat 1.94g

Sodium 65mg

Potassium 159.3mg

Calcium 87mg

Iron 1.03mg

Vitamins (Vitamin C total ascorbic acid; B-6; B-12; Folate-DFE; A-RAE; A-IU; E-alpha-tocopherol; D; D-D2+D3; K-phylloquinone; Thianin; Riboflavin; Niacin)

Calories 54

44. Pumpkin pie protein shake

Ingredients:

1 cup of pumpkin puree

1 cup of skim milk

1 tbsp of brown sugar

2 egg whites

1 medium banana

1 small green apple

1 tsp of cinnamon

Preparation:

Separate the egg whites from yolks. Peel and grate the apple. Cut banana into small pieces and combine the ingredients in a blender for 30-40 seconds. Sprinkle some cinnamon on top and leave in the refrigerator to cool for a while.

Nutritional values for 1 glass:

Carbohydrates 11.36g

Sugar 8.03g

Protein 10.23g

Total fat 3.87g

Sodium 79.43mg

Potassium 208.1mg

Calcium 104.9mg

Iron 1.89mg

Vitamins (Vitamin C total ascorbic acid; B-6; B-12; Folate-DFE; A-RAE; A-IU; E-alpha-tocopherol; D; D-D2+D3; K-phylloquinone; Thianin; Riboflavin; Niacin)

Calories 72.7

OTHER GREAT TITLES BY THIS AUTHOR

www.ingramcontent.com/pod-product-compliance
Lightning Source LLC
Chambersburg PA
CBHW071748080526
44588CB00013B/2189